The Phoenix Living Poets

ENTERING ROOMS

Poets Published in
The Phoenix Living Poets Series

★

ENTERING ROOMS

By

JOHN SMITH

CHATTO AND WINDUS

THE HOGARTH PRESS

1973

Published by
Chatto and Windus Ltd
with The Hogarth Press Ltd
42 William IV Street
London W.C.2

★

Clarke, Irwin & Co. Ltd
Toronto

ISBN 0 7011 1925 X

© John Smith 1973

Printed in Great Britain by
T. H. Brickell and Son Ltd
The Blackmore Press, Gillingham, Dorset

For

BETTY MULCAHY

INCOMPARABLE SPEAKER

To believe in God is not a decision that we can make

SIMONE WEIL

NOTE

Acknowledgements are due to the editors and publishers of the following periodicals and anthologies in which most of the poems in this volume first appeared: *Workshop, Poetry Review, Northwest Review, Contemporary Review, Tribune, Borestone Mountain Poetry Awards, Poems from Poetry & Jazz in Concert,* and to *Poetry Now* (B.B.C. producer George MacBeth).

CONTENTS

Prologue

First, as you enter the room, you will be aware
Of one thing only: the colour of the walls, the floor, the ceiling.
It will be white, unglaring, and of an eggshell finish.
You will find it unnerving though not unduly ominous.
To begin with it will seem not so very dissimilar
From rooms you have entered before. These, however,
Will rarely, if at all, have been white under your feet.
The texture of these white surfaces will be uniform.
As you adjust to this you will also become aware
That the door by which you entered has totally merged
With the white wall. And that there are no windows.

The next noticeable thing will concern your own person,
Or rather the clothes in which you are dressed. They have become
White like the room and completely encase you
In a suit of what might be white polystyrene.
Of course you are unable to see your face or the back of your head
And that causes you some disquiet. Especially you wonder
About the colour of your eyes. You begin to blink rapidly.
These small moments of non-whiteness do not comfort you.
Apart from yourself the room will at first seem empty,
But that is illusion. You will discover, more by sense than sight,
That it contains an object: a small white cube.

Curiously enough you will at first refrain from touching it
Though unaware of the reason. You will kneel down
And gaze upon it for a long time. Because there are no shadows
You will not at once discover that it possesses a small groove
Encircling it some one and a half inches from the top.
Not until you touch it with your fingers will you know this.
So it may be a box, a box with no fastener.
However the lid, if it is a lid, refuses to lift,
Though refusal, for such an inanimate block, is a word
Too human and personal; say, rather, it will not move.
Therefore it may be merely a solid cube of wood.

Again you are at fault, for you have no possible means
Of telling from its whiteness the substance of which it is made;
Its weight is no guide. Nor, when you shake it, does it rattle.
You will spend a long time manipulating this cube
Though you will not know whether it is a second or a year.
You will be unaware of the usual functions of the body.
It may be that you will carry it to various places
Within the silence of your room. Silence?
Ah, that is another thing; you will begin to confuse
The whiteness with silence. When that happens
You will not know whether you have seen colour or heard a sound.

Immediately you will begin to wonder
Whether anything happened or not. You will wait
Concentrating your entire being on the situation.
Was there noise? Was there colour? You will return.
You will replace the cube in the exact position
From which you removed it. You will back to a wall.
If a door has opened you will not know. Except:
There has been a change. Has there been a change?
It is a pity there is no one you can discuss it with
Though it is doubtful whether any conversation
Would move you a degree nearer to understanding.

First, you will be aware, entering the other room,
If indeed you have entered, of one thing only:
The colour of the walls, the floor, the ceiling,
Will be textureless black. You will examine your body
Though you will be unable to see your face or the back of your head.
In the exact centre of the room you will discover. Yes.
Oh, and by the way, please don't worry yourself about the names
We use when we try to baptise God. Eventually you will move
To a wall where a door may open or may not open.
You may listen, if you wish, hoping that God might speak.
But that, of course, is a very different matter.

To Find Myself

Walking to find myself in the obsolete city
It is easy looking at my reflection in shop windows
To think those apparitions are the answer.
False ghosts! What can they reveal?

My suede shoes splash in the puddles, taking me
Each evening on a feverish cold search.
Perhaps the pigeons under the false front of St. Paul's
In Covent Garden know me, yet are forbidden to tell.

I shall walk up the steps of a magnificent hospital
And give myself into the care of surgeons:
Those white coats, those lost and bandaged faces.
I shall request the pleasure of their knives.

They will lay me without concern or gentleness
But in the improbable elegance of naked humankind
On a table; I shall not cry out, but merely contemplate
With a devoted wonderment, how their instruments dazzle.

They will peel back my skin, pare the pulsating flesh;
The smallest bones, even in the little finger
On my left hand, shall not escape their meticulous joy.
But for what? Supposing, at last, they should say,

Unwinding their no-faces, bland in disbelief,
Not: 'here we have found this tumour, here that fault'
But, marking their graphs in secret, delicately observe:
'We are sorry, we can find nothing, nothing, nothing, nothing, at all.'

Wouldst Eat A Crocodile

When I was a boy I occasionally lived in Africa,
Mostly in summer on Sunday afternoons
When the assegais and the pampas grass
Stretched in an endless missionary-eating plain.

My eyes would squint in the heat, and the fever-swamps
Would draw one side of my face in a deadly ague.
At the height of the sun I would shout in delirium
Staggering with thirst, but the pools were full of leeches.
Considering the number of tigers I killed
It is not surprising that in Africa they do not exist.

Remembering those days I am prompted to ask a question,
Though you need not answer it if you find it embarrassing.
It is this: Have you ever been bitten by a crocodile?

I detect from your silence that slight unease of guilt
Which indicates your lack. It is an experience, believe me,
Not easily forgotten. But I blame no-one but myself.
My bearers? I scorned such upperclass aboriginal appendages.

No, Ladies and Gentlemen, even when you are indulging
In your most luxurious vices, such as hunting,
Or making love, reviling your relations, or merely
Listening, as one does, to Poetry or Jazz, remember
You can live safely only one impossible life at a time.

But to return to my crocodile, my wound.
The day was exceptional and my genius ripe;
The plains of Africa glistened, only, remote in the azure sky
The vultures hung, heavy with the digestible flesh of missionaries
Happily devoured, listening with the abrasive ecstacy of their kind
As I began with profound and reverent passion to play
The opening of the Beethoven piano sonata op. 111.

It was then that it happened. More terrible than vultures,
Out of a sky blue as the eyes of Mozart the foul beast dived, and
SNAP! Ah, where was Beethoven then?

How long I lay there suffering in the grass I do not know
Nor whether Stanley or Livingstone lifted my bleeding body
And stanched my wounds; it does not matter. But to this day I wish
I had known the name of that excellent crocodile,
My mentor and friend, most proper enemy.

I did not die, as I hope may be obvious;
But what of that beast? I have walked more warily since
In the Africa of my adulthood, in the feverish plains
Of London, through the assegai teeth of the world
Where missionaries smile, comforting as chocolate.

But sometimes, on an underground stairway, my wound throbs,
So that I lurch and clutch the rail that is always moving,
And the people disappearing forever into the past or the future
Are shocked, seeing those teethmarks red on my breast.

I do not want them to stop, with their righteous zeal,
Offering words like lint and bandages, ambulances of concern.

As the crocodiles swarm in for the kill with their swivelling eyes
And their teeth, yellow as the keys of Beethoven's piano
Jangling on the plains of Africa, for what, Ladies and Gentlemen,
        must we call?
But for the terrible useless protection of God alone.

You Also, Narcissus

Shrugging the crumpled tissue of the night
Away from my face, who lies in the bed beside me?
What welcome given in some ecstatic hour
Turns in the cold morning to rejection and distate?
Well at last this lover is dead and cannot speak.
But what shall I do with the corpse?

The trouble is there is always too much time
To learn how to cope with old liaisons: this rigid man, for instance.
He will lie there, snugly, while I labour through the day,
When I smile, when I drink. And not for many nights
Of electric blankets or cosy hot water bottles
Will the warmth thaw or shift him.

He will lie there contemptuously smug in his abandoned beauty—
Well, hardly beauty; vanity is the least of my vices,
And if not young then *younger*, which is intolerable.
For it is not the sitting room, nor the kitchen, not the usual offices,
But the bedroom that is the private necropolis
Of one's dead selves; the bed their grave.

One leaves no lover with such despair, I do assure you,
As one leaves each brief sardonic decade
The old young men. They are like dolls
With their vacant predatory stare and their pink limbs
Which cannot move of themselves but continually reach out
With their little piping memory voices: 'like this, like this'.

So he will disgust and fascinate me, seductive long in my bed;
Until, after many a change of sheets, one night he will vanish.
I shall turn back the cover, which is like earth under snow,
To find no mocking corpse but flowers growing:
Flowers the colour of my ageing eyes; and, heady with their scent,
With what fresh rapture shall I turn to kiss the pillow.

If You See What I Mean

The man has a glass eye; it
    Has looked unwinking at me for the past hour
Watching me drink. I sit
    On a hard seat in a pub, the beer sour
In my stomach, and stare;
A man with a glass eye lolls, gazing back at me there.

A finger apart, the other eye
    Promiscuously flutters about the myopic bar
Flitting, settling like an obscene black fly
    On the exposed flesh whisky has left ajar,
And the secrets oozing in regret.
At the corner of the glass eye the skin, by the nose, is wet.

It is not a tear. The blind,
    Believe me, are no more compassionate than the sighted,
And why, for Christ's sake, should a half dark man be kind
    Staring implacably at a life blighted
By more than a snatched out
Jelly, or a simple doubt?

I could lean over now and knock
    That glass egg skittering among the stools,
And laugh at the gaping hole, and the shock,
    The flesh-whitening, sweating terror of the poor fools
Choking on alcohol. Or lean
And offer him both my eyes. If you see what I mean.

Death at the Opera

Is this what death is like? I sit
Dressed elegantly in black and white, in an expensive seat,
Watching Violetta expire in Covent Garden.
How beautiful she is! As her voice lures me toward her death
The strings of the orchestra moisten my eyes with tears,
Though the tenor is too loud. Is this what death is like?
No one moves. Violetta coughs; stumbles toward the bed.
Twenty miles away in the country my father is dying.
Violetta catches at her throat. Let me repeat: my father
Is dying in a semi-detached house on a main road
Twenty miles off in the country. The skull is visible.

I do not want it to end. How exquisitely moving is death,
The approach to it. The lovers sob. Soon they will be wrenched apart.
How romantic it all is. Her hand is a white moth
Fluttering against the coverlet of the bed. The bones
Of my father's hands poke through his dry skin.
His eyes look into a vacancy of space. He spits into a cup.
In a few moments now Violetta will give up the ghost;
The doctor, the maid, the tenor who does not love her, will sob.
Almost, our hearts will stop beating. How refreshed we have been.
My father's clothes, too large for his shrunken frame,
Make him look like a parcel. Ah! The plush curtains are opening.

The applause! The applause! It drowns out the ugly noise
Of my father's choking and spitting. The bright lights
Glitter far more than the hundred watt bulb at home.
Dear Violetta! How she enjoys the flowers, like wreathes,
Showered for her own death. She gathers them to her.
We have avoided the coffin. I think that my father
Would like a box of good plain beech, being a man
From Buckinghamshire, a man of the country, a man of the soil.
I have seen my father, who is fond of animals, kill a cat
That was old and in pain with a blow from the edge of his palm.
He buried it in the garden, but I cannot remember its name.

Now the watchers are dispersing; the taxis drive away
Black in the black night. A huddle of people wait
Like mourners round the stage door. Is this what death is like?
For Violetta died after all. It is merely a ghost,
The voice gone, the beautiful dress removed, who steps in the rain.
Art, I conceive, is not so removed from life; for we look at death
Whether real or imagined, from an impossible distance
And somewhere a final curtain is always descending.
The critics are already phoning their obituaries to the papers.
I do not think God is concerned with such trivial matters
But, father, though there will be no applause, die well.

Resurrection Song

The paving stones on fire in fire
   In fire on fire the bush of spring;
From the wrecked windows and the doors
   The risen dead lean out to sing.

The stone leaps up and paints its mouth
   Where the grave sky kneels down to kiss;
What human calendar could predict
   That Time would stitch a time like this?

The golden oriole of the sun
   Flies through the sweet enfranchised sky
Where the arabian moon reflects
   His passion in her lucent eye;

And every sandgrain on the shore
   With miniature and angelic voice
Wakes with a psalm the obsolete sea
   And bids the exiguous spray rejoice;

While in man's labyrinthine mind
   New words like flames of wisdom start,
God with transfigured tongue proclaims
   The final eloquence of the heart.

A Man of the New World

Not from a body stretched beautifully upon a body
Enclosed by passionate arms enclosed by arms in turn
Did my unquick substance soon to be live flesh leap,
Nor in rich heats of love did my true self burn.

I came silent, numbered, numbed in a cold wilderness
In a phial labelled with my father's name;
And without violence or ecstacy, is it small wonder
That I see in a glass darkly an image of two men's shame?

From such engendering I shied away,
A deprived person stumbling in a depraved world.
Nevertheless at moments in that groping
I found a small part of my whole self in my part self curled.

I fell into distress, into the munching jaws
Of a steel trap that wrenched my bones apart;
It was the first of my deaths. A generous science
With steel and plastic offered a new start.

My eyes, alas, rusted in disrepair;
Perhaps my benefactor was less blind than me.
But when I open his pupils wide in the sun
I worry sometimes whose is the world I see.

Now my own heart is eating out its grief
In a place removed while I suffer another's ache.
In the appalling dark of man's worst dilemma,
Dear God, when at last I die, whose heart will break?

Something To Do With Faith

Exceptional moments do not necessarily require
Words for their celebration. They can go
Off after extravagance in quite drab attire;
It is not demanded they should make particular show.
Sometimes they are quiet, small—indeed, yes, very small—
And often only to one person known, if known at all.

They need not be witnessed. Say a shaft of the sun
Should glance on mica in a unique way;
It might be observed or not; it would be just one
Of those things. But the glory as the light flashed that day
Would be what I mean. Or as, for a fraction of a second, a violin
Might wake its dark wood from death and let the green life flow in.

The petal could fall from a rose, or it could not fall.
There is no making up the moment that shows us the face of God.
It does not command our presence; it exists. That is all.
Paradise, presumably, will be paradise whether trod
By man or not; useless to think its excellence depends
On the will that conceives it, or that it serves human ends.

More tranquil than our silence is the inscrutability of God.
Does he smile when we speak? When in pride we deny
His existence does He, perhaps, with polite gravity nod
His unimaginable head, looking down on us with the same wry
Glance of a Humanist philosopher amused that man should opine
In the face of incontrovertible evidence, a belief in the Divine?

Fidelity

Take no offence, love, if I shift
My eyes from you to someone else
And find along another's glance
Mysterious quickening of the pulse;

Or lie within another's arms
And feel a different body press
With curious passion on my own,
My mouth accept a stranger's kiss.

Fidelity is what we are
And needs no action to confirm:
Whoever's breast I weep upon
Yours is the heart I keep from harm.

I Saw the Face of Him I Loved

I saw the face of Him I loved
    Gaze from a thicket of fire,
His head within those scorching flames
    Bound by a coronet of briar,
His eyes as clear as the ice in May
    That frosts the bluebell on its spire
But in his adamantine gaze
    No passion or desire.

And stretching out my hands I ran
    Toward that bush of flame
But the loud words within my heart
    My live mouth could not frame
When down to that tree of crimson then
    All the small carroling song-birds came,
I heard from gold and silver beaks
    The naming of the Name.

I saw the face of Him I loved
    Like sun motes in the air
Like the miraculous catherine wheel
    That burns in God's eternal fair;
More luminous than a red giant's eye
    Flamed out his mane of dazzling hair,
But nothing, nothing I saw of love,
    Grew in His passionless stare.

And stretching out my hands I ran
    Toward that glittering space,
But nothing of substantial form
    Could my wild arms embrace;
When through the electric landscape then
    I saw a delicate white deer pace
And wept to see that fabulous beast
    Dancing before His face.

I saw the face of Him I loved
    Look up from a grave stone,
And threw my harsh self headlong down
    Where the encompassing weeds had grown,
But could not, though their poison stripped
    My live flesh from the bone
Reach to that passive countenance
    But wept there alone,

As you must, when you see His face
    In fire, in air, in stone.

Thoughts from Torcello

A waterbus plies the tourists to the island:
Its name is holy. I am speaking of course
Of the island, not the boat, though that is irrelevant,
For it is not the object that matters but the fact
Of consecration. The island is uninhabited
Except for the figures who people the mosaics;
It is not known how they obtain their sustenance
Nor in what grave language they converse.
When visitors arrive they remain implacably silent.

They nest in the dome and arches of the church
In a mode of violent stillness. Outside, the vines,
Withering in autumn, let the grapes decay.
The grass is rank. The angel on the left
Has wings of black gold, the drapery of his shift
Seems the material substance of God; his scythe is deadly.
The winnowing of men by flood, by plague,
Disturbs the air no more than the faint haze
Wrought by the wings of gnats above the river.

Time has distributed the liberal flesh
Of the sometime human; the drowned and swollen bellies
Steamed in the prodigal energy of the sun
Five hundred shadowless years behind our backs.
But the beings in the dome, along the walls,
Keep their androgynous and hieratic shapes,
Or if one crumbles, splintered under the sharp,
The ineluctable eye of a pitiless God,
The fragments, hard as maize, lie where they fall.

The sprawling body of a dead man soon decays,
And though sometimes we weep is it not kind
That wind or waves or fire or the eating earth
Ravage that useless substance? The penance
Suffered by Angels whether contrived or real
Is their endurance: to see beyond Time
Illimitable years devoid of passion and love,
Knowing more sharply the cold condition of God
Whose algebraic nature scorns man's nescience.

No scouting traveller with his camera's jaws
Nibbles away those fifty thousand dead,
But in apalling duplication hauls
Even the ghosts of these harsh artefacts
To flicker and writhe on a thousand vulgar walls
As the real Cherubim or Seraphim
Within the mouths of priest and chorister
Suffer perpetual despoliation
Their bright shapes dulled by the spittle of mankind.

Night draws a soiled sheet over the island's ribs;
The tourists have departed leaving a thin scarf
Of luminous petrol that blinks up at the sky
From the edge of the lagoon. In the smart hotel,
Over the curious, unfamiliar drinks,
Will one with no warning feel his limbs go cold
And stare in terror out to that hallowed place
Not knowing who will shrive him of his sins:
God's holy vampire or the unregenerate dead.

On Motril Beach

On Motril beach the urchins snare the birds:
Delicate sea-skimmers, their plumage brighter than spray.
The traps are simple: thin wire between two sticks;
The lure, a small sardine (how the flesh tempts us).
The boys wait silently, brown as the brown sand,
Till the birds dive and are tripped, then leap, their hands
For a moment swifter in the air than wings,
And the feathered creatures are caught, though not to be killed;
Not yet. First, with exulting glee, the boys
Flaunt the sweet trophies then neatly break their wings,
Bending them backward with peculiar grace
Till the bones snap. The birds are silent, but the boys laugh,
A warm and endearing sound, as only children
(Whom we must not corrupt) can. As Christ said: 'Suffer them'
But again, inexplicably: 'Not a sparrow falls'.

There are various games to be played with living creatures
Whether men or birds (One nigger more or less,
Another Jew). The boys (whom God loves) throw
The maimed birds in the air like shuttlecocks
That fall and flutter lumpishly in the sand. Sometimes
In that incongruous element the urchins scoop
Small shallows and bury them up to their gaping beaks;
The legs, of course, being very fragile, break.
Or two might, playing antagonists, thrust their catch
Like quivering lances at each other's eyes.
One six year (innocent) unwittingly
Clasps to his breast like a tiny Albatross
A shredded bird, not cognizant of the cross,
And beats it against the rib-cage of his chest
Where a heart, I suppose, beats like that bird, inside.

(In Seville, where the crippled beggar lay,
A breathing gargoyle, reaching for arms, I paused
Dropping a coin, but longed to spit in his face,
Unwind his festering stumps and claw at them
But Society forbade, and, doubtless, God.) But, those birds:
You must hear the end of this gentle comedy.
Tied by their claws to string, like toys they are whirled
In a breeze that, curiously, scarcely ruffles their feathers.
Small specks of blood (like Christ's?) stream in the firmament
While shadows begin to blunder about the beach
As an hour (perhaps the ninth?) drags forth the dusk.
The tide is turning and the sea grows cold.
Squabbling amongst themselves the boys depart
Clutching the scuffed birds in their scrubby hands.
Later, in their hovels, they eat them. That is good.

In a Curious Way

It is not easy to kill fish.
When you drag them up out of the water
You have first to extract the barb from their throats.
Sometimes it will have been swallowed so deep
It will lug the guts up with it;
Even so the fish will not quickly die.
It is perhaps no misfortune that they are dumb
And have such expressionless faces;
It might be disturbing if you could hear their screams.
But even their eyes do not signify. They are like
The eyes of certain Ikons I have seen in Serbia
Which are recorded, in the high style, as 'inscrutable'
Though meaning in ordinary, low, common language, merely 'blank'.

You must not suppose at this juncture that I am adopting an attitude
Of disapproval or rebuke. After all do I not, fastidiously
Dissecting them with a silver fish-knife and fork, comment on
the flavour?
Their flesh is on the blade. I have been told
That when you first hoist them out of their wetness your hand
Is to them like a glove of red hot emery paper; their scales are seared.
But I have to eat, no less than you. I have read somewhere in an
encyclopaedia
That only the angels and archangels subsist in eternity without food,
And I recollect also that on some of those Ikons the wings of the angels
Were irridescent and not unlike the scales of certain fish.
Do my blasphemies, I wonder, scorch and blacken those mystical
beings
Which, in a curious way, would seem to resemble the Angel Fish
of Japan
Or those veiled and silent gliders off the coast of Java?

You would be wrong to castigate yourselves for tearing those gills.
Did not Christ, after all, distribute miraculously substantial fishes
To the gathered multitude? For indeed God cannot live by prayer
  alone,
And many men have been distributed and devoured,
Dragged first out of the air by some invisible hand;
That is certainly undeniable. But I suspect you are thinking
With all this talk of fish and angels that I pursue
Some intricate pattern through which I shall lay bare a moral.
You should keep your thoughts to yourselves; or else do not blame me
If you are disappointed. There are no threads to gather up:
Poems, like actions, should be sufficient in themselves. Nevertheless
It may be worth remembering in the rising and spawning summer
That you have recourse to God when you feel the hook in your mouth.

St. Jerome and the Lion

Somewhere it is perhaps possible: a man
    Sitting at ease in a landscape, by his side
    A lion; the man, his intellectual pride
Fallen away at last, the lion's ferocity
    Calmed. I have seen paintings of this
    And scorned such visions of unattainable bliss.
But now I begin to conceive that there may be, in Time,
    Such a landscape; in a the fury a pause:
    Conflict, in justification of the laws
Of science, reduced to an immovable peace.
    Above, a cloud floating with exact purpose in the sky.
    The climate temperate, the air warm and dry.

Nevertheless the nature of the lion
    Is different from the saint's. Our error
    Lies in supposing that because beauty partakes of terror
Terror partakes of beauty. It is not so.
    Of the possible rage of the beast, yes,
    The saint may discover some element to confess,
But he cannot confront the lion in its passion,
    Nor can that tame beast hope to know
    The exalted peace of the saint, or grow
Holy like him. They merely inhabit themselves
    Each being consumed by an inviolable fire,
    Distinct, perfect, the essence of their desire

Which is the province of God. For they rest
    In His inscrutable mind which is the ground
    Of love. Hence their calm. They are bound
By the exquisite and invisible chains of his perfection
    Within the compass of forever. The beast
    And the holy man are brought to the same feast
Wherein they devour and are devoured by God.

Order prevails beyond justice; nothing conspires
To harry the saint's mind, beast's blood, with urgent desires.
The name of the saint is Jerome; the lion is nameless.
To what purpose does God, I wonder, direct
Such parity of being? What thought does he perfect?

The Blood of God

It's raining, and the cold air
Coils round my body like the moist pulp of a cucumber,
Not the green skin, but that almost colourless flesh
Which bleeds a fine lymph when you cut it with a knife.
I am told my own blood is crimson and surprisingly thick;
How noiselessly it runs through the tunnels of my earth.
If I cut myself it would spurt out. It would not be diluted by rain,
This cucumber dampness. Why do I think of blood on this rainy
    morning?

What colour is the blood of the trees? They feed on rain.
Some they suck up with their roots which are like veins;
Some they absorb through the pores of their leaves.
My hands are riddled with pores, and I have seen
The foliage of certain tropical plants quite like my hands.
I do not suck up blood, nor drink it through my skin.
I keep the rain out. I will not have my red blood
Turned into a pale river pink as my fingernails.

Cucumbers taste like rain. That is why you eat them
With such relish, such voluptuous pleasure, in summer;
Blood, I think, is a winter luxury.
It is very warm, but it is clearer and purer then.
If this rain were to turn to blood—and I have heard of a prophecy
'A rain of blood'—it would be warm and sticky.
I should not like that; the idea fills me with revulsion.

Do you not think God is an extraordinary creature
Communicating his desires through such ambiguous means?
Whenever I cut anything, I wonder, does he bleed?
What is the colour of the blood of God?
Is it cold? Is it hot? I have heard some people fancy
That rain is the tears of God, that water is love,
That love is water. But maybe it is His blood.

Not one Martyr in the whole history of Christendom
Was drowned by the pale, cold, cucumber drizzle of rain.
Not one. Their blood always spurted out; their veins were severed.
I have prayed, but I have not been chosen.
You do not believe me. *I have prayed*. Look. Look.
My eyes are brimming with rain. And my blood
Is so cold, is so cold, is so cold.

Thinking About Death on the Road to Sfax

Thinking about death on the road to Sfax,
The monotonous journey from nowhere into nowhere,
I enter the perilous cavern of my skull
Which is like the tortuous labyrinth of Matmata
While the black desert and the contiguous sky
Fill my starved belly with the fermented grain of Time
On which we are weaned and which is our Grave's manna;
For the disease we die of is the disease of birth
Which Henna cannot wash out with its blood
Nor the pagan Christian transplant of a heart
From whose first principle springs a second cause.

How strange that in the thickness of our world
We cannot see those slits which are cut for us,
Thin holes through which we must walk, white emptinesses.
And yet with what fastidiousness are they fashioned
Being tailor-made for our individual shape
Since we cannot wear the clothes of our neighbour's death
For, like the abandoned flesh, the soul is particular,
And the spirit also, unique as a fingerprint.
It is how we don that space, that transparency
That must concern us. Each gesture that we make
From our gross structure models the Grace of our death,

Which does not eat us like a ravenous beast
But rescues us from dying, whether we fall
Through a blaze of air, or in an empty room
At the tide of summer drown in our own breath.
And here, in a green place, on the road to Sfax,
Lie many dead, named and unnamable,
Tended more carefully than the anxious living,
Watered like flowers, though they will not blossom again.
But who would wish to see the ghost of a face
However loved, bloom in the vitreous air,
Dazzled by sunlight, deafened by new words?

My meditation throbs in its dark, though the sun
Whiter than salt spices the feverish day,
Till a spark bites at an edge of thought, and my skull
Blazes with molten death. But a richer flame
Flares in the skull of God within whose furnace
Like Southwell's babe the dead are vivified
With Heraclitian fire. That energy renews
The root of being, and here, on the road to Sfax
In an English cemetery, purifies and redeems,
While behind in its clot of sand El Djem decays;
Before, the port of Tunis chokes on its rust.

The Berber drums the satellite from the sky;
The dancer leaps up when the machine is broken
While no sirocco with its rasp of sand
Rages more fiercely than Man's spirit rages
In ceaseless animation; so the incongruous gates
Of this small cemetery clang shut on nothing
For the ground is merely bones; no worth lies here.
Thinking about death on the road to Sfax
I see the world as a carapace for life
A husk of seed, an egg out of which we break
To become what we are. *Things* perish: that is all.

Epilogue

Having travelled a great distance and through experience
Of various comfortable or uncomfortable methods of transport,
One day soon, say in perhaps a thousand or fifteen hundred years,
You will find—most of the colours draining away from your eyes—
That you are standing at the very edge of a flat, yellow square,
Gritty, uncompromising; essentially the kind of place
Most likely to be avoided, yet unaccountably desired.
You will recognise this as the growing point of your journey.

But before you can place one of your feet, or even so little as a toe,
Onto this square—which, incidentally, extends so far that the horizon
Seems to be poised almost directly above your head,
You must divest—forgive the slight anachaism—divest yourself of
  your clothes:
The overture to *Don Giovanni*, for instance, the *Dichterliebe*,
Poems of Andrew Marvell, veils of Cranach and Paul Klee,
And those ambiguous white beaches peopled by Henry Moore.
For the time being, however, you must retain your own somewhat
  irritating flesh.

It will wither soon enough. The excoriating wind
That howls like the sirrocco from the thin blue line of the sky
Will scrape it as a cheap file grates down the fingernails;
But you cannot merely lay it to one side. Memories of course
Must go. That process is more desperate. Remember those martyrs
Who, of all exquisitely unimaginable tortures were flayed,
Their skin, thinner than the screams to whose ludicrous accompani-
  ment
It was peeled away, offered far less excruciating pain.

You will survive the loss. The names of a few people, or
If you have been extravagantly fortunate perhaps one only,
Will lodge like a stone in your throat; you will choke on it.
But in the end even that must yield, must be spewed out.
And who would have thought your eyes could remain so dry?
Had you turned round before you would have witnessed nothing
Of that exodus, that parade. But now,
At this moment of nothingness, what visions, what multitudes!

With such a grotesque intensity of desire your whole being
Will urge itself forward, but you will find that your feet
Not so much as one centimetre will encroach onto that sand.
Wait therefore. The longing will subside until, looking down,
What astonishment! Already behind your heels you will observe
A band of yellow fine as a long blond hair.
It will rise up. Like the balled fist of a legendary God
It will smite you; like the jawbone of an ass.

Your clenched teeth will fly apart; your mouth
Will open in a great blackness, but not to scream.
It is not for me to prophesy the sound you will utter then,
What syllables will rise like a gush of spiritual blood
Drenching the vitreous air. Your arms thrust out
You will topple onto that vast plain of implacable ochre like a tower.
Nor can I tell you what voice may echo in that wilderness.
I will say to you only: *The mountain is there. Climb it.*